yes mum

yes mum

wit and wisdom for your mum

edited by jo ryan

Published in the United Kingdom in 2010
by Tangent Publications
an imprint of
Axis Publishing Limited
8c Accommodation Road
London NW11 8ED
www.axispublishing.co.uk

Creative Director: Siân Keogh
Editorial Director: Anne Yelland
Designer: Simon de Lotz
Production Manager: Jo Ryan

ISBN 978-1-904707-91-2

2 4 6 8 10 9 7 5 3 1

Printed and bound in China

about this book

This inspiring collection of amusing animal photographs and witty, relevant and thought-provoking quotes and phrases is the ideal book to let your mum know how you feel about her. It offers words of wit and wisdom written by people of all ages for sons and daughters to offer to their mums as a way of saying "I love you" or simply "Thanks". In today's fast-paced world, it's easy to take everything mum does for granted. This book is the ideal way to show your mum just how much she means to you.

about the author

Jo Ryan is an editor and author who has been involved in publishing books and magazines across a wide variety of subjects for many years. From the many hundreds of contributions that were sent to her from parents and their children from all over the world, she has selected the ones that best sum up what being a mother is all about.

If mum's at home,
everything goes well.

A mother who
is really a mother
is never free.

A mother's heart is the child's schoolroom.

Being a full-time mother is one of the highest salaried jobs since the payment is pure love.

He that would the daughter win
must with the mother first begin.

Mothers are tied to their children
by compassionate bonds.

Every great man had
a great mother.

Everything I am
I owe to my mother.

A mother is the
only person on
earth who can
divide her love
among ten children
and each child still
have all her love.

Everything worthwhile
I have done in my life,
I owe to my mother.

My mother's heart was
so large that everybody's grief
and everybody's joy found
welcome in it.

A mother isn't a person
to lean on, but a person to
make leaning unnecessary.

A mother needs courage, fortitude, flexibility, firmness and patience.

Mothers know how to tie bows, fit baby-shoes and string together pretty words that make no sense.

Mothers reflect God's
loving presence on earth.

A mother is the golden glow of lamps, the firelight on a hearth.

A mother's pleasure is the
happiness of her family.

The heart of a mother is a deep abyss at the bottom of which you will always find forgiveness.

Motherhood requires an intense love by the mother, yet it must help the child grow away from the mother and become fully independent.

Motherhood is the
keystone of the arch
of matrimonial happiness.

My life began with waking up
and loving my mother's face.

No man is poor who
has a good mother.

Mother: the most beautiful word on the lips of mankind.

Where there is room in the heart, there is room in the house.

No gift to your mother can ever
equal her gift to you – life.

My mum was as
gentle as a dove…

…and as brave as a lion.

The noblest calling in the world is that of mother.

A mother's love is
like a circle…

…it has no beginning
and no ending.

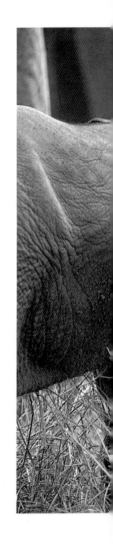

True motherhood
is the most beautiful
of all arts, the greatest
of all professions.

Youth fades, love droops,
the leaves of friendship fall…

…a mother's hope
outlives them all.

One generation
plants the trees…

…another gets the shade.

A mother is the greatest, strongest and most lasting teacher her children have.

A man loves his sweetheart
the most, his wife the best,
but his mother the longest.

A mother's children are portraits of herself.

There's no way to be a perfect mother, but a million ways to be a good one.

My mother's prayers have clung to me all my life.

Mum is here and mum is there, but most important she's everywhere.

There is no path
so flowery as that
imprinted with my
mother's footsteps.

A mother is someone who dreams great dreams for you, but then she lets you chase the dreams you have for yourself and loves you just the same.

Sometimes the poorest woman leaves her children the richest inheritance.

Angels can fly
because they take
themselves lightly.

A mother's love is mighty.

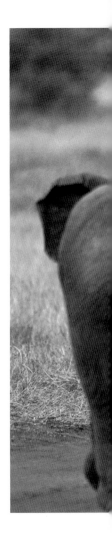

Motherhood is a
partnership with God.

My mother's teaching is
all I started out with.

A mother's love need not be acquired, it need not be deserved.

Mothers hold their children's hands for a short while, but their hearts forever.

No language can express
the power and beauty and
heroism of a mother's love.

My mother is the kind of person that I one day hope to be.

A mother's love enables her child to achieve the impossible.

Mothers hear things
without listening.

A mother is the one
who is still there when
everyone else has
deserted you.

Only mothers can think of the future since they give birth to it.

Anyone who doesn't miss the past never had a mother.

Rejecting things because they are old-fashioned would rule out the sun and the moon and a mother's love.

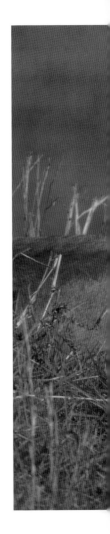

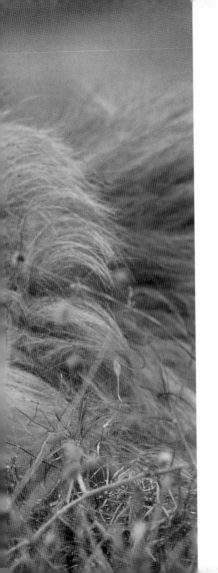

Mum, you banish
the clouds of
darkness and
make peace
return to my heart.

Mum's voice is the only one worth being heard.

A mother is the person you hurry to when you are in trouble.

We never know the love
of our mother until we
become parents ourselves.

A mother's love is peace.

Home is where my mother is.